A Gift For:

....

From:

....

How to Use Your Interactive Storybook & Story Buddy™:

1. Activate your Story Buddy™ by pressing the "On / Off" button on the ear.
2. Read the story aloud in a quiet place. Speak in a clear voice when you see the highlighted phrases.
3. Listen to your Story Buddy™ respond with several different phrases throughout the book.

Clarity and speed of reading affect the way Cooper™ responds.
He may not always respond to young children.

Watch for even more interactive Storybooks and Story Buddy™ characters.
For more information, visit us on the Web at www.Hallmark.com/StoryBuddy.

Copyright © 2011 Hallmark Licensing, Inc.

Published by Hallmark Gift Books,
a division of Hallmark Cards, Inc.,
Kansas City, MO 64141
Visit us on the Web at www.Hallmark.com.

Editors: Emily Osborn and Megan Langford
Art Director: Kevin Swanson
Designer: Mark Voss
Production Artist: Dan Horton

ISBN: 978-1-59530-354-7
KOB8001

Printed and bound in the United States

Hallmark
GIFT BOOKS

BOOK 3

Cooper's
Bedtime

By **Stacey Donovan** • Illustrated by **Crista Couch**

Every night when it was time
to go to bed, Cooper wanted to
stay up and play, instead.
He didn't want to brush his teeth
or wash his face, and he certainly
didn't want to get under the covers.

The only part of bedtime
he liked was when his mom
tucked him in and said,
"Cooper, I love you."

So one night when Cooper's mom said, "It's past your bedtime,"
he thought that maybe he hadn't heard her right,
so he kept on playing with his army bears.
"Hey, little soldier," she said. "Time for bed."
Cooper thought that maybe she was talking to somebody else.
But then he heard her again.
"Cooper, go to bed."

Cooper tried to close his eyes,
but they kept opening again.
He could hear the TV in the living room,
but he couldn't tell what show it was.
He listened and listened.
It sounded like a show about robots!
Were they scary robots? Or smart,
nice ones that would help you with
your homework? Cooper bet they would
be nice! He just had to know
for sure what was on TV.
Cooper had a great idea!

Cooper decided to go check
it out for himself.
If he was very, beary quiet,
his mom wouldn't hear him
get out of bed. He tiptoed down
the hall so he could see the TV.

It was just the boring old news that his mom
    and all the other grown-up bears liked to watch.
He thought about how much better the news would be
        if they had a story about dinosaurs.
Especially if they were real dinosaurs, stomping around
    and surprising all the birds in their nests.
        Cooper's mom looked up and saw him.
        She shook her head and said,
            "Cooper, go to bed!"

She kissed him goodnight,
and Cooper tromped to his room again.

As soon as he got under the covers,

Cooper heard a car vroom by the bedroom window.

He didn't know who was in it or where it was going.

He wondered and wondered. Maybe it was . . .

. . . a car full of tigers, driving to a night circus!
Maybe an elephant truck would zoom along next—
or even a car full of clowns!
If he stayed in bed, he might miss seeing
all kinds of circus performers!
Cooper did NOT want to do that.

He went to the window to watch the road.
After a while, a bus appeared,
but he couldn't see who was inside.
Maybe they were rock stars driving to a concert!
He climbed on the nightstand to get a closer look,
but he knocked the clock to the floor with a noisy thud.
His mom opened the bedroom door and said,
"Are you up again? Cooper, go to bed!"

So Cooper's mom kissed him
goodnight one more time,
and he slunk back to bed.
He heard her turn off the TV,
and after a while, he heard
a whirring noise.
What was that?
He listened and listened.
It sounded like . . .

. . . a spaceship landing right in his front yard!
Maybe aliens would come out! Were they mean aliens?
Or nice ones who took you on spaceship rides?
Cooper bet they would be nice.
If he stayed in bed, he'd miss his
one and only chance to meet them.
Cooper did NOT want to do that.

As he snuck toward the door, Cooper's mom
came into the living room and said,
"Young bear, what do you think you're doing?"
"What's that noise?" he asked.

"It's just the washing machine," she told him.

"Why can't you stay in bed, for bee's sake?"

"But what if something fun happens?" asked Cooper.
"I don't want to miss anything!"

"I see," said his mom. "But, Cooper,
what if something exciting happens in your dreams?"

Cooper had to think about this.
He thought and thought.
Could he be missing some exciting dreams?
Cooper did NOT want to do that.

Finally, he said, "Mom, you're right.
I could be missing a good one right now!"
"Now go to sleep," she said, "and in the morning,
I'll fix you a bowl of your favorite honey."
Cooper got under the covers. His mom tucked him
in, gave him one more good-night kiss, and said,
"Cooper, I love you."

Cooper wondered what his
dreams would be like.
Maybe he would be on a pirate ship,
sailing far away to an island
with roller coasters and Ferris wheels.
Maybe he'd meet some dinosaurs and robots
and aliens, and they'd all be very nice.
And with all that fun waiting for him
in his dreams, Cooper fell asleep.

IF YOU LIKE STAYING UP LATE JUST LIKE COOPER™,
WE WOULD LOVE TO HEAR FROM YOU.

Please send your comments to:
Hallmark Book Feedback
P.O. Box 419034
Mail Drop 215
Kansas City, MO 64141

Or e-mail us at:
booknotes@hallmark.com